Couple Care

Liya Lev Oertel

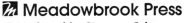 **Meadowbrook Press**

Distributed by Simon & Schuster

New York

Library of Congress Cataloging-in-Publication Data
Oertel, Liya Lev.
  Couple care : the best advice from happy couples / Liya Lev
Oertel.
      p. cm.
  ISBN 0-88166-431-6 (Meadowbrook) ISBN 0-743-22856-1 (Simon
  & Schuster)
    1. Man-woman relationships—Popular works. 2. Couples—
    Popular works. I. Title.
  HQ801 .O315 2002
  306.7—dc21

                                              2002006989

Editorial Director: Christine Zuchora-Walske
Copyeditors: Kathleen Martin-James, Angela Wiechmann
Proofreader: Megan McGinnis
Production Manager: Paul Woods
Art Director: Peggy Bates
Cover Photo: DiMaggio/Kalish, Corbis Stock Market

Published by Meadowbrook Press, 5451 Smetana Drive,
Minnetonka, Minnesota 55343

www.meadowbrookpress.com

BOOK TRADE DISTRIBUTION by Simon & Schuster, a
division of Simon and Schuster, Inc., 1230 Avenue of the Americas,
New York, New York 10020

06 05 04 03 02   7 6 5 4 3 2 1

Printed in the United States of America

Dedication

To Jens, for giving me the best relationship I could
have ever hoped to have, and for teaching me
how to keep it that way. I am still learning,
so thank you for your patience.

Acknowledgments

Thank you to all the people who shared their stories and experiences to make this book possible:

Sharon and Ken Adamson, Polly and Mark Andersen, Sara Anderson, Pete and Teri Aumann, Virginia and Michael Bailey, Anne Boyd and Ron Anderson, Joni Berg, Jane Davidson and Joseph Gredler, Myra Denin, Peter and Charlotte Donnelly, Michelle Rolfs Dunbar and Ross Dunbar, Cyndee and Matt Elumba, Sabine Grundmann, Mark and Cory Gunderson, Genarose and Jeffrey Hohertz, Bill and Vicki Knapp, Stephanie Wank Kofman and Ilya Kofman, Brad and Alisa Lacomy, Paula Lev, Lynne Medgaarden and Ross Scott, Brad and Alina Maxwell, Eric and Rebecca Messinger, Cindy Miller and Sean Beaton, Carl and Irmgard Oertel, Jens Oertel, Martina Oertel and Jürgen Ketelhut, Dana Ott and Norris Stenson, Ann Parker and Bill McConachie, Christie and Chris Patka, Tom and Ruth Rolfs, Alla Simkin, Iosif Stern, Renee and Jeff Stoebner, Camille and Jerry Thompson, Leslie and Kyle Tidstom, Penny and Tom Warner, Angie and Josh Wiechmann, Danielle and Matt White, Christine and Ron Zuchora-Walske, and to all of you who chose to share your experiences and wisdom anonymously.

Contents

Introduction

Many people believe the song that says, "Love is all you need." On the contrary, you need more than love to create and keep a meaningful, loving relationship from the first date to the fiftieth anniversary and beyond. Along with love, you need communication, diplomacy, romance, equality, support, respect, and acceptance. All 150 pieces of advice in this book are based on those seven components. And if you follow the advice, your relationship can't help but thrive.

I have the good fortune to be married to a man who wholeheartedly has my best interest at heart, respects me as an individual, and wants me to be happy. But is our relationship perfect? No, and I don't know of any relationship that is. While writing this book, I spoke to over one hundred people who are dating, recently wed, married for decades, divorced, or widowed. I had the privilege of learning from their successes and mistakes. Writing this book helped me see that my relationship needs more than love, and I hope reading it will do the same for you.

Best of luck to you,
Liya Lev Oertel

Chapter One

Communicate, Communicate,
Communicate, and Then
Tell Each Other How You Feel

The Art of Listening

Learn and practice the art of listening. Pay attention. Be interested. Be supportive. Comment appropriately. Appreciate the sharing.

When we were newlyweds, my wife and I had great conversations late into the night. But several years and several kids later, we noticed our conversations didn't have that same magic. I thought it was because we no longer had interesting things to say, but my wife said it was because we'd forgotten how to be good listeners. We used to look in each other's eyes, sit close, and hang on to every word as if it were gold. We didn't just tune each other out while we waited impatiently for our turn to talk; we listened intently and encouraged each other to speak. It was easy to talk for hours when we listened with such respect. That night, we decided to put those listening skills back into effect. Our conversation didn't last all night, but it reminded us why we fell in love years ago.

—Marcus, married eleven years

I Told You So...

If you can't delete it from your vocabulary, then limit saying "I told you so" to no more than three times a year. "I told you so" benefits no one.

ᗡ

Years ago I had an opportunity to buy a luxury car in a deal that seemed too good to be true. Even though Nia was reluctant, I went ahead with the purchase. When the car turned out to be a lemon, I had to explain how I had been easily separated from my money. Ten years later, even when I know I've royally pissed off my wife, she has never mentioned the incident or tried to make me feel like a lesser man for my gullibility.

—Malcolm, married ten years to Nia

My sister felt it was her duty to predict and then gloat over every mistake I made as a teenager. Consequently, I came to think of "I told you so" as the scum underneath the grime at the bottom of the barrel. Even though my husband and I infuriate each other occasionally, I've always appreciated that we help each other when we use poor judgment rather than use the opportunity to assert our superiority.

—Nia

Bite Your Tongue

Everybody's entitled to an opinion. Don't try to talk your partner out of his or hers just because you disagree.

♡

I support the theories that an opinion isn't wrong just because it's different from mine and that two different opinions can both be right. It's the practice that takes loads of work because I think I'm right all the time. (Jens and my mom would be happy to confirm this.) So I have to bite my tongue to keep from pointing out what I think is the error of Jens's ways. I think I'm getting better, because my tongue has fewer and fewer teeth marks in it with each passing year!

—Liya, married eight years to Jens

Move On

Not everything needs to be discussed and ana-
lyzed for hours. Sometimes it's sufficient to
acknowledge the difference of opinion and move
on. As they say, don't make mountains out of
molehills.

*While we were still dating, we wasted many hours
on rather insignificant conversations, analyzing the
details of anything said or done. (I'm afraid I was
significantly responsible for this.) Before we got
married, Chris's sister gave us a piece of advice that
shortened these lengthy conversations: Choose your
battles. When we start to disagree or begin to dwell
on little details, we always ask ourselves, "Is this
battle worth fighting? Would it make any difference
if we just ended the conversation and moved on?" If
the answer is no, one of us will usually pull the
other into a hug and say, "Let's not talk about this
anymore." Normally, we end up laughing about
how silly the conversation was in the first place.*

—Christie, married two years to Chris

Keep Talking

Encourage each other to talk about your days, interests, and work. It's one of the best ways to show that you're interested in each other's lives.

When we first met, I was fascinated by Udo's interests, hobbies, and work, so I was perfectly happy to discuss things he wanted to discuss. Unfortunately, when I felt we should talk about my work and hobbies as well, he wasn't interested. The one-sided pattern we established suited him just fine, and he saw no reason to change it. This lack of interest made me feel as if I were an unimportant part of the relationship, and after a while, the relationship no longer felt like a relationship.

—Sabine, separated after five years

Mind Your P's and Q's

Be polite. *Please* and *thank you* really are magic words.

ᗡ

In these days of road rage and what seems to be a slide into general incivility, please and thank you have so much to offer. We see politeness as a form of respect, a way of saying, "I recognize you as a person." And of all the people in the world, one should certainly offer such courtesy to one's life partner! Whether we're at the dinner table or racing around at 8:00 A.M., trying to get everyone out the door, please, thank you, *and* you're welcome *make the family machinery roll a little more smoothly. Of course, there are times when, in the panic of the moment,* please *flies out the window. ("This diaper's leaking all over the rug! Get me a towel, quick!") But once the moment is over, there's always time for* thank you. *An added bonus for being courteous partners: polite kids!*

—Ann and Bill, married fifteen years

Finish Your Own Sentences

Don't complete your partner's sentence, even if you know how it'll end.

❤

I used to think it was sweet when a couple knew each other so well, they could complete each other's sentences. Then my wife started doing it to me. Sure, most of the time Judy knew what I wanted to say, and it's nice that she knows me that well. But I wanted to complete my own sentences. Sometimes I felt as if she were stealing my thoughts and words instead of using her own. So I told her how I felt. As I figured, Judy thought she was just being helpful— saving me the trouble of saying something she understood right away. We made a deal that she'll stay quiet one out of every two times she wants to jump in before I'm finished talking. Now she hardly finishes my sentences at all—unless I lose my train of thought or can't find the right words. Then I rely on her understanding.

—John, married eighteen years to Judy

Wait Your Turn

Don't interrupt, even in an argument. Wait your turn.

◊

My husband is the type of person whose mouth moves faster than his brain. This causes him to speak before he thinks—or before I'm through speaking. It usually takes me five minutes to relay a two-minute tale because I have to pause for his interruptions. It's especially frustrating when he interrupts me during an argument. I never feel as if I get my fair say. One day I got fed up, so I tried an experiment. I started a conversation, waited for his interruption, and then interrupted him right back. I know two wrongs don't make a right, but in this case, it got his attention. We interrupted and reinterrupted each other so many times, we started to laugh. It lightened the mood and gave me a chance to tell him how I felt about being interrupted.

—Asa, married two years

Think Before You Criticize

Next time you're about to correct or criticize your partner, ask yourself if the criticism is really necessary. Will either of you learn something valuable from the comment, or will you simply diminish your partner's dignity while sounding like a pompous know-it-all?

ᗡ

At work, we learned that before you criticize, you should ask yourself whether the problem affects performance or morale. If it doesn't, you should keep quiet. If it does, you should use constructive criticism. Talk about the behavior and its impact, and ask for suggestions on how to fix it. I decided to try this at home. It worked in two ways. First, I learned to consider what I could do to improve a situation before voicing any criticism. Second, if a talk was necessary, I could explain my position with less emotion, which made it easier for my husband to understand.

—Anne, married eleven years to Ron

A Spoonful of Sugar...

Sometimes a complaint or a criticism is necessary, and sometimes you simply can't hold your feelings in. In either case, coat your concerns with honey so they're easier to swallow.

When we complain to each other, we try to do so lovingly and with a bit of humor to make it easier to swallow. For example, "I really love you, but if I have to watch one more football game, I'll boot you through those goalposts."

—Myra, married two years

Don't Sweat the Small Stuff

Make a point to leave three unpleasant things unsaid each day. (This rule should be applied mainly to the little things that aren't really worth complaining about.)

ᗡ

As I was putting away the dishes my husband, Jens, had washed, I noticed a pot was still dirty. Meanwhile, Jens came home from the store without the diapers I had asked him to pick up. Shortly thereafter, I realized that the laundry was still in the washer, even though Jens had passed by the machine several times. My mood was, to say the least, sour. Then I remembered that Jens got up with our early-bird toddler every weekend so I could sleep in—because he loved me. So when he asked me why I looked upset, I told him I had decided to say nothing. He pointed out that saying nothing while looking gloomy was not terribly helpful. I promised to cheer up. Then we went to the zoo and picked up some diapers along the way.

—Liya, married eight years to Jens

Body Language Speaks Volumes

Often, it's not what you say but how you say it that counts. Never use body language to imply that your partner's a moron and you're a martyr for enduring his or her stupidity.

ᗡ

While Jenny assured me that she didn't think I was stupid, her whole body shouted otherwise. The resigned sigh and slump of the shoulders, the upward tilt of the head and the pursed mouth, and, worst of all, the eye rolling. She made me feel two inches tall without saying a word. And I couldn't argue, because she'd simply insist she had never said anything insulting (which was true) and that it was all in my imagination (which was false). I guess those gestures made her feel better about herself. They kept her from having to invest much in the conversation or the relationship. And they effectively ended the conversations—not to mention our relationship.

—Jason, divorced after fifteen years

From Work to Home

Build in some transition time between work and home so bad feelings from one don't spoil the other.

We used to come home and begin complaining about whatever hassles we might have had that day—work, clients, coworkers, the commute. Often the first words we exchanged were negative, and that set the mood for the whole evening. Now, we agree not to mention anything work-related for at least ten minutes after we get home. Instead, we take the time to change clothes, hug each other, and otherwise make the transition from work to home in a positive way. By the time those ten minutes are up, all the negative stuff from work doesn't seem so bad—and it certainly doesn't seem bad enough to spoil an evening.

—Polly and Mark, married eighteen years

It Never Hurts to Wear a Helmet

Think before you react. A humorous, understanding, or neutral reaction can defuse a potential problem, while a defensive, angry, or irritable reaction can incite an argument.

ᗡ

In college, I spent an evening helping Josh edit a long research paper. It was an exhausting experience, but the paper was in great shape when we finished. The next night I came home and there sat Josh, wearing his replica St. Louis Rams football helmet. He quickly blurted out, "Can you read over the paper again?" As I imagined spending another night reading that paper, I felt angry words rise up in my throat. But Josh looked so ridiculous in his helmet, I couldn't speak. I had no idea why he was wearing the helmet. Apparently, he wanted to distract me (or symbolically shield himself). The helmet forced me to think before I reacted. So instead of getting angry and starting a fight, I laughed and agreed to read through his paper one more time.

—Angie, married four years to Josh

Just Listen

Be a neutral sounding board when your partner needs to work things out of his or her system.

ᗡ

After eight years of marriage, I learned not to offer advice when my husband was "sharing" his work issues. Not only was he not receptive to my input, but he also believed I was telling him what to do because I thought he couldn't handle the problem on his own. Now I simply listen and ask if there's anything I can do. He usually says he just appreciates my listening. As a result, we no longer feel misunderstood and resentful after these conversations.

—Anne, married eleven years to Ron

When Martina returns home from her job with her eyes clearly stating she wants to be left alone, I sit next to her, kiss her nose, and give her time to open up. The ice breaks before long, and she starts to talk. I don't criticize or try to be a wise guy. I just listen and let her control the conversation. All she wants at that point is to talk to somebody who cares. So I comfort her and wait until she is more relaxed before I offer a second opinion (if she asks for it).

—Jürgen, together nine years with Martina

Not a Dumping Ground

It's one thing to share what's on your mind; it's another to dump your frustration on your partner. Find other ways to vent your anger.

ᗡ

I tried to be sympathetic when my husband vented, but that just encouraged him. If I tuned him out, he accused me of not caring. Finally I told him that I'd set a ten-minute limit on his monologue. If he needed more time, he'd get ten additional minutes. He huffed silently until something set him off again. I timed him and after ten minutes asked if he needed ten more. He began to laugh. Since then, he still vents, but he's often done before the time's up.

—Sally, married eighteen years

Whenever one of us has to vent, we visualize everything that's upset us, go into an enclosed space, and let out a loud scream. This releases our negative energy and thoughts and also makes us laugh because, well, it's a strange thing to do. We call it "primal scream therapy."

—Maggie and Christopher, married twenty-one years

Most Partners Aren't Psychic

If you don't ask for it, don't get upset if you don't get it.

♡

When we were first married, Laura used to set up tests for me in her head: "If he really knows, loves, respects, and cares for me, he'll do this task." She'd get upset while she waited for me to read her mind, and if I didn't, she'd do the task herself, all steamed. This was a no-win situation that upset us both. Finally, I pointed out that I wasn't an insensitive, lazy bum just because I couldn't read her mind. She agreed and now tries to ask when she wants something.

—Joseph, married seven years to Laura

I used to feel as if I were nagging if I had to ask Joseph to do things. I still feel that way a little, but he assured me that he doesn't think of it as nagging. While his help still means so much more when I don't have to ask for it, I try hard to get past that and simply say what I want. We have been arguing much less and are getting more done cooperatively, so the effort is worth it.

—Laura

Don't Assume

You know what happens when you assume: You underestimate your partner and usually work yourself into a lather over nothing. Get the facts first.

ᗡ

When I'm angry, my instinct is to clam up and wait for my husband to figure out what he has done to upset me. He's usually clueless, which further aggravates me. I've learned that disagreements end more quickly when I address the issue right away— especially when the problem is based on something I mistakenly assumed. For example, when my husband told me about a business convention in Las Vegas, I got angry because it sounded as if he had already decided to go without consulting me. "Isn't it nice that he doesn't even have to consider who will watch the kids?" I thought. Then I remembered my rule: Don't hold it in; talk it out. "What about me?" I asked. "Does that mean I get to go on a trip when you get back?" He looked at me in surprise and said, "I don't want to go to Vegas without you." Well, it's a good thing I decided to talk about it!

—Virginia, married six years to Michael

It's Okay to Say No

It's better to say no than to resent saying yes.

♡

During the first few years of our marriage, I was afraid that if I said no to my in-laws, they wouldn't like and accept me. So I went to all the family functions and helped with moves, renovations, and numerous other projects. Sometimes I was happy to help, but not always. I resented feeling as if I couldn't refuse, and I silently blamed my wife for my resentment. One day I finally lost it. My wife was completely surprised and assured me that no one would think less of me if I didn't always agree to help. I felt a little silly for letting this resentment cloud my feelings for my wife, and I've been saying no to her family periodically since then. Nobody has disowned me or treated me coldly as a result. Now when I say yes, I always mean it. That helped my feelings toward my new family and my wife improve tremendously.

—Steve, married four years

Tactful Truth

Honesty is the best policy, but a little tact also goes a long way. Truth comes in various forms, so choose the one that best fits the situation. Honesty never suffers from thoughtfulness.

When we have a dinner engagement and my wife is getting ready, she always asks how she looks and whether I like what she's wearing. Although she wants me to be honest, she doesn't want me to be brutal. So to play it safe, I prefer to ask for some options. This way I can say I like one outfit better than the other.

—Brad, married seventeen years to Alina

I Love You, But...

Don't send mixed messages. If you have something positive to say, don't dilute it with a negative qualifier.

When I'm happy, I say so. My wife, on the other hand, never used to say she was happy. She was "happy but..." Something always made her happiness incomplete. Life was great...but it would be better in a new house. Our child was really smart...but he needed constant stimulation. The day was beautiful...but there was so much to do inside. This really bothered me. I kept thinking I wasn't doing enough to make her happy. When I told her how I felt, she was honestly surprised. She didn't realize what she was doing. Since then she has really tried hard to catch herself before she qualifies any positive statements. I've now heard her say several times that she's happy. Just happy and nothing else.

—Jens, married eight years to Liya

Go to Bed Early

If you do most of your catching up in bed before falling asleep, go to bed a little earlier.

ᗡ

Every night after our son has fallen asleep, we give each other foot massages in bed before we go to sleep. We both look forward to this time when we get to pamper each other and chat without any interruptions. In addition to talking about what we did that day, we also share our dreams and thoughts about the future.

—Renee and Jeff, married two years

Chapter Two

ʗ

Lose the Brass Knuckles:
Fight a Clean Fight

Of Course I'm Right!

You can always be right or you can respect and understand your partner. The need to "win" every argument will slowly but surely damage your relationship. Loving and respecting each other is more important than winning an argument.

♭

When we have a discussion (that some people might call an argument), my natural inclination is to point out how right I am. But as I became aware of the necessity for tolerance in my marriage, I stopped trying to be the "right" person. Instead, I've tried hard to understand what Mark experiences from his point of view.

—Polly, married eighteen years to Mark

Our experience has shown us that we can become overwhelmingly resentful if we both focus on how we've been hurt. Of course we're both right and we've both suffered injustice from the other! But problems aren't resolved by both people being right. Rather, they're resolved when you understand the validity of each other's feelings and when you move forward together from that understanding.

—Mark

You're Not Perfect

Be responsible for your own actions. Always try to recognize and admit when you're wrong.

♡

We're so busy with work and kids that we've become accustomed to making quick decisions, sometimes based on incomplete information. Once I made a social arrangement, only to have my wife say, "You agreed to go on Thursday? But we have soccer on Thursday!" Sure, I could have defended my decision by insisting, "No one told me we had soccer on Thursday" or by making some other excuse that prevented me from being wrong. But to what end? Instead, I've tried to look at things from my wife's viewpoint, which has helped me recognize and admit when I might have made a bad decision.

—Brad, married seventeen years to Alina

Forgiving the Unforgivable

Accept an apology gracefully.

♡

About two years ago, I did something I thought was unforgivable. I was dusting the knickknack shelf— my most hated chore—and I tried to do it as quickly as possible. In my haste, I accidentally knocked off Keisha's prized possession: an heirloom vase her grandmother had given her. It shattered on the floor. I didn't think she could possibly forgive me. At best, I thought she'd say she forgave me, but then she'd scream at me, give me the silent treatment, or insist on breaking one of my things to even the score. When Keisha walked in, I told her what had happened. She was silent, then she started to cry. I told her I was sorry. I wanted to turn back time or magically put the vase back together, but all I could do was apologize. After a few minutes, she finally said, "It's okay." She was still crushed, but somehow she found the strength in her heart to forgive me— truly forgive me, without screaming, turning a cold shoulder, or wanting revenge.

—James, together with Keisha seven years

       Couple Care

Remember When...

Once you forgive a mistake, don't bring it up again. If you're preoccupied with past grievances, your life will have no joy.

My parents were married fifty-five years. They had a pretty good relationship, but as long as I can remember, my mom brought up the same grievance during every argument: "Remember when you overturned my washtub when you were mad?" Although I never overturned any washtubs throughout my marriage (of course, we had washing machines instead of tubs, and those are harder to overturn), I'm sure I did plenty of other things that my wife could have thrown in my face. She never did, though. I was always grateful for that.

—Iosif, widowed after forty-seven years

Fight for a Reason

Always fight for a reason, not for the sake of fighting itself. If a fight won't produce anything productive, stop and save your energy for one that will.

ᗞ

My sister calls my marriage abnormal because my husband and I never fight. The truth is, we rarely fight. When we do, our fights are more like heated discussions. We don't engage in senseless yelling or door slamming. If we reach an impasse in our discussion, we stop, walk away, and readdress the issue at another time.

—Teri, married six years to Pete

I secretly look forward to our fights. Although they're usually intense, we always have a better understanding of each other after them. And when all is said and done, I feel closer to my wife.

—Pete

I'm Dizzy

When fighting, stick to one issue at a time.
You'll never put out a fire if you keep adding
fuel, and you'll never resolve an argument if you
keep adding grievances.

♡

*I'm guilty of switching topics when we argue. One
time while arguing with my boyfriend about how to
put away the groceries in our fridge, I somehow
turned it into an argument about who does a better
job cleaning the house and who has the strongest
work ethic. I even started in on how his friends
spend too much time at our house. (Don't ask me
how I got off on that tangent.) Dominic followed
me from topic to topic for about a half-hour, then he
stopped and said, "Wasn't this fight about groceries?
You've got me turned around so many times, I'm
dizzy." Since then, whenever I go off on a tangent
when we argue, all Dominic has to do is act dizzy to
get me back to the topic at hand.*

—Luisa, together five years with Dominic

Apologize First

Sometimes an apology can defuse anger, put things in perspective, and keep an argument from getting out of hand.

♡

When we first got married, we learned a trick that has helped us incalculably: In an argument, the one who's least upset apologizes first. Why? Because it's easier for that person to do so. When you're very upset, it can be almost impossible to apologize. But if your partner apologizes, your anger deflates almost immediately because you feel understood. Then both of you can move on to the resolution phase.

—Mark and Polly, married eighteen years

Don't Spark Another Fire

When you're angry, try not to spark your partner's anger, too. Two angry people can't hear each other.

When John irks me, my tone of voice changes. He hears it and stops talking, and I go for a walk. That avoids doubling the problem—it keeps me from saying words in haste that would spark John's anger on top of mine. During that time-out, we both think about the thoughts, feelings, or actions that irked me. When we get together, John listens first, and then I listen. When I irk him, I listen first.

—Barbara, married forty-five years to John

I Can Hear You

Yell only in case of an emergency, such as a fire. Yelling suggests a lack of control, which will usually lead to words and actions you'll later regret.

My husband is half Italian, and I realize his tendency to say everything at the top of his lungs may be genetic. Still, it bugs me. So when he's getting a little too voluble, I say quietly, "Honey, I can hear you just fine." He knows exactly what I mean and that I'm not mad—just getting a headache—and he takes it down a few decibels.

—Christine, married five years to "Ronzo"

Go to Sleep as Friends

Don't fall asleep angry with each other.

♡

When my brother died suddenly of an asthma attack in the middle of the night at age twenty-nine, the first thing his wife said to me was, "I didn't kiss him good-night." No matter what our problems are, Cyndee and I always resolve to kiss good-night or say "I love you" before we go to sleep. I wouldn't want to spend my last moments being too stubborn or too tired to tell my best friend that I love her.

—Matt, married four years to Cyndee

Recognize That Person?

Look at each other when you argue. Eye contact implies that you're actually listening and not just pretending to do so. Also, when you make eye contact, you'll find it more difficult to throw out hurtful accusations.

I think I could write an entire book on how to argue. Essentially, you must argue with respect. Your partner isn't your moral or intellectual inferior just because his or her opinion or perspective is different from yours. Eye contact helps you recognize that your "opponent" is the same person to whom you make love.

—Myra, married two years

Sometimes Fighting Is Funny

You'll fight, and that's normal. But if you try to see the humor in fights over silly things, you'll fight less and laugh more.

While doing the dishes one night, Josh decided to let a greasy frying pan soak. After filling it to the brim with water, he returned it to the stovetop, splashing a little water along the way. I couldn't help but imagine him dumping the entire pan when it was time to retrieve it. I moved the pan to the counter because I thought it would be safer next to the sink—and therein lies the irony. When Josh went to slide the pan into the sink, it capsized and flooded our open silverware drawer. Immediately, an angry barrage of "Why are you so clumsy? I moved the pan so you wouldn't dump it!" and "Why did you move the pan? I put it on the stove for a reason!" poured out. Just when a full-blown fight was imminent, we looked at the silverware all but floating in the drawer, and we couldn't keep straight faces. We realized it really wasn't worth a fight, but it definitely was worth a good laugh.

—Angie, married four years to Josh

No Name-Calling

Words like *stupid, idiot, moron*, and other insults should never cross your lips when talking about your partner.

ↁ

It took me ten years to realize that my husband's favorite hobby was to make me feel dumb. He constantly called me names and belittled my efforts at self-improvement. When it became clear to me that I wasn't a "ninny" after all, I packed up and left. We tried counseling, we dated for a while, but I always thought in the back of my mind that he didn't really love or respect me. He spoke more compassionately and lovingly to our dog.

—Monica, divorced five years

Think Before You Speak

Don't say whatever comes to mind in the middle of an argument. Censor yourself. Say only what's relevant, and avoid saying simply hurtful things.

My wife, Irene, was wonderful about evaluating her words before they came out of her mouth. I, on the other hand, am one of those people who shoots first and asks questions later. If something's on the tip of my tongue, there's no holding it back. Over the years, Irene's wisdom kept us together. However, my lack of wisdom subtly altered our relationship. It was a general feeling—she trusted me a little less, maybe even respected me a little less. Looking back on it, I wonder how she could have been so patient and loving despite the loss of trust. And now I would give so much to have bitten my tongue at least once to save her a painful moment.

—Iosif, widowed after forty-seven years

Do It—Or Else

Offer choices as opposed to issuing ultimatums.
An ultimatum can have only two outcomes:
Your partner either obeys your will, usually with
anger and resentment; or your partner suffers
the consequence, which hurts you both.

♡

*"If you don't go to this party with me, I'll have
headaches every time you are in the mood for the next
month." "If you go out with your friends tonight, I
might not be here when you get back." You name it, I
heard it. I don't know why my then-wife thought
threatening me was the only way to get what she
wanted. I told her if she would just ask me I'd do
what she wanted if I could. In the first years of our
marriage, I gave in to her threats—to keep peace, to
make her happy, to avoid a problem. But after a
while, I stopped caring. The more she threatened, the
less I wanted to give in. Finally, when she told me,
"If you leave the house, you don't have to come
back," I left and didn't come back.*

—Adam, divorced after five years

Learn from Your Fights

Pay attention to your arguments. If you notice you have the same argument regularly, try to restructure it to change the outcome and prevent the argument from recurring.

This may sound silly, but we frequently used to fight about what my husband wanted to wear when we'd go out. He was something of a free spirit, while my tastes were more conservative. So when he'd put on an outlandish outfit, I'd automatically argue that he couldn't possibly wear it out of the house—certainly not with me, anyway. We'd have a big fight, he'd wear what he wanted, and both our moods would be spoiled before we even left the house. Then I noticed if I acted casual and made some humorous comment about his appearance, he tended to listen. Because he didn't feel as if I were forcing him, he frequently changed into something else. We'd both be pleased with the outcome and enjoy the evening instead of fuming all night.

—Alla, widowed after thirty years

Time-Out

Sometimes it's not *what* you're arguing about but *when* you're arguing that creates the problem. If you feel the time isn't right for an argument, call a time-out.

♡

We used to argue while getting ready for work in the mornings. Even if we resolved the issue, the argument was fresh between us so we'd still be angry at work. Now we set a time—7:30 A.M.— beyond which we're not allowed to argue. If we're not done, we write the gist of the argument and say nothing about it until we get home. Because we write it out, neither of us feels as if we're giving in. A hug, a kiss, and an "I love you" remind us that we really do love each other and can get past this. We pick up the argument when we get home, but much of the anger has melted out of it by then, so we usually work things out pretty easily.

—David and Kiersta, married eleven years

Grump on a Stick

Learn to spot the dark clouds over your head. If you know you're in a bad mood and are likely to pick a fight as a result, warn your partner. Then try to lighten up so you can share a good mood with your partner instead.

I recently purchased a cardboard frowning face glued to a large Popsicle stick. It's called "Grump on a Stick," and it's hysterical when held in front of your face. I used it to apologize to my husband after I'd been in a particularly bad mood. The humorous acknowledgment of my own grumpiness shifted the emotional tone of our home instantly.

—Myra, married two years

Try Another Perspective

Before you get upset, put yourself in your partner's shoes. Seeing the situation from his or her perspective might change your own.

I like things neat, and I used to get irritated when areas in our house were cluttered. Then I realized that Sharon feels more at home when things are a little out of order. For example, one day I got mad at her because there were papers around the nightstand on my side of the bed. Then I suddenly stopped myself and said, "You're 'nesting,' aren't you?" We both laughed and she said, "I never looked at it that way, but that's how I feel."

—Ken, married twenty years to Sharon

Not in Public

Never criticize each other in public. It humiliates both of you and makes others uncomfortable in the process.

♡

Looking back on my marriage, I know this is something I did a lot to my husband. I frequently felt the need to point out in front of others how wrong he was, how stupidly he was behaving, and so on. More often than not, my comments provoked a heated response that escalated into a bitter argument. This certainly didn't improve anybody's mood or self-respect. I knew I should have kept my mouth closed, but often I couldn't stop myself. My husband died of cancer a year ago. I sure wish I could have stopped myself when I had the opportunity.

—Alla, widowed after thirty years

Chapter Three

♡

Don't Forget You're Lovers

Don't Drift Apart

In your relationship, you began as a pair and you should end as a pair. Don't put your partner on hold while your children grow up or you focus on your careers. Otherwise, you may not have a relationship left by the time the kids leave home or you retire.

I saw many couples drift apart and stop being, well, couples because they were too busy with other things. When we had kids, I saw that we were in the same danger. So I made it a priority to spend some quiet time alone with my husband every weekend, even if only for an hour. Grandparents or friends fill in with the kids, and then Gary and I go for a walk or even just coffee—anything where we can hold hands and look at each other.

—Chris, married sixteen years to Gary

As the kids came, we had little time for each other. The fact that my wife always made some time for us reassured me that I didn't come last in her affections.

—Gary

Distraction-Free Zone

Real romance is practically impossible amidst daily family chaos. Establish a distraction-free zone away from kids and to-do lists, where you can give your partner your undivided attention.

Our kids always liked to sleep with us, even as they got older. So we established a "not before midnight" rule. That's the time we catch up with each other. And if we feel like being romantic, we know we're safe for those hours. If we don't do anything by midnight, it's safe to say we won't need any privacy after that.

—Michelle and Ross, married fourteen years

Light Your Fire

Don't forget you're lovers as well as parents, homeowners, professionals, and so on. Find little ways to show each other you haven't forgotten.

♡

I think it's important to let your husband know you remember your sex life. My favorite thing is to light candles to set the mood—and to hint to him that I'm in it!

—Cyndee, married four years to Matt

Make Time to Make Love

Arrange your schedule so it best suits your love life. Find time to make love leisurely and in peace.

ᗡ

I always felt sex without noise was like riding a bike without a seat: You get there, but you don't really enjoy the journey. Ever since we adopted a twelve-year-old, we've felt that sexual noises are inappropriate in the home. So our intimate time can be less restrained, we encourage our son to spend time with friends at their homes, and we schedule our love life accordingly.

—Anne, married eleven years to Ron

Turn Off the TV

Find a way to keep yourselves from automatically reaching for the TV remote. It might encourage you to reach for each other instead.

We bought an entertainment armoire, so the TV and remote control are hidden behind doors. This way, instead of automatically turning on the TV when we sit down, it has to be conscious decision. Since then, we've watched television significantly less and have talked more, read more, and caught up on some accumulated paperwork. It's like getting a few extra hours a day as a present.

—Robert and Liza, married thirteen years

Take a Good Look

Make eye contact at least three times a day. See eye to eye with the person you share your life with.

ᗡ

Out of curiosity, I decided to see how often Nelson and I actually made eye contact. I picked the week-end because we were both home. It was amazing. We made eye contact that lasted more than a second only once during the two days. Sure, we looked at each other, but not eye to eye. Throughout the weekend, we were too distracted by other things. We certainly acted lovingly—holding hands during a walk, exchanging run-by kisses, and cuddling on the couch while watching television—but no eye contact! Not too long ago, it seemed, we used to gaze at each other all the time. What a change a few years and a few kids made! After that, I made a conscious effort to slow down a few times a day and look directly at my husband. And that makes me feel closer to him.

—Judy, married fourteen years to Nelson

The Wonder of a Walk

Take walks together and hold hands.

♡

Our courtship was a series of walks, and walking hand in hand remains a part of our married life. Taking a walk has a certain excitement, like a mini-vacation. It's a quick escape from mundane chores. Walking together lets us talk without distraction as our minds and feet wander. Some walks have enabled us to clear our heads and reach major life decisions; others have simply provided the thrill of a discovery. On one of our late-night walks while Stephanie was pregnant, we discovered an open door at a local wholesale bakery. Taking a walk to buy midnight pastries became a weekly event, which we continued as a family after our son was born.

—Ilya, married six years to Stephanie

Couple Care

Make a Date

Go on dates regularly, even if you've been together for years—especially if you've been together for years.

My husband and I have a standing date every Saturday. We treat it as an unbreakable appointment to be cancelled only in cases of real emergencies. The baby sitter is booked, and we go out, even if we don't have any specific plans. Even a movie or a cup of coffee together is a luxury, and it reminds us that we're still a couple.

—Karen, married eight years to Larry

Cut a Rug

Go dancing once in a while. Few things are as romantic as holding each other close and letting your bodies move to music.

I'd say the only thing I'd change about my husband is that he doesn't like to dance—or that he doesn't like to dance in public. I, on the other hand, would go out dancing every night if I could. But I don't want to drag Jens to go dancing because I know he won't have fun, and so, by extension, I won't either. However, every once in a long while, he suggests it himself, and we go. He concentrates on the pleasure I get, ignores all those people who are supposedly staring at him, and has a good time. More than the dancing itself, I love Jens for enjoying it with me. The rest of the time, we clear the toys out of the way, turn up the music, and dance around the living room.

—Liya, married eight years to Jens

Save Your Pennies

Save up for a romantic evening by contributing to a special container every night. Once the container is full, go out and have fun spending it on each other.

Every evening we empty all our change into an old candy tin. When the tin is full, we cash it in at the bank and go on an hors d'oeuvres crawl, visiting several places to sample fun drinks and appetizers and just to enjoy each other's company. Collecting the money builds anticipation, and that's all part of the fun.

—Christine, married five years to Ron

Bowl of Ideas

Make a list of romantic activities that require little or no preparation, and keep it handy for those times when you and your honey need a little inspiration.

♡

On paper strips, we write romantic activities, such as dining out, taking a walk, going for a scenic drive, having a picnic, reading poetry to each other, taking a bubble bath together, giving each other a massage, dancing in the backyard, stargazing, and so on. We keep the strips in a special blue bowl prominently displayed in the kitchen. When we feel like doing something romantic but don't know what, we just pull an idea out of the bowl.

—Darlene and Frank, married fifteen years

Vacations for Two

Take vacations as a family and take vacations from the family—just the two of you—to help you remember why you fell in love in the first place.

Ross and I take mini-vacations to reconnect with each other. We'll spend a weekend at a Civil War reenactment or a historical library. The total change from our everyday lives helps us get away in mind and spirit. In the evenings, we find a hotel with a pool and a hot tub, and we focus on each other. I think the busyness of everyday life intrudes on couples' love lives, and they forget one of the things that attracted them to each other in the first place: being lovers. For me it's important to take the time to really focus on Ross and let him know how special and important he is to me.

—Lynne, married six years to Ross

It's the Little Things

Make small, unexpected gestures to show your affection and love every day.

ᗡ

Cyndee always surprises me with gifts under my pillow or "I love you" cards in my suitcase. One day I came home late, feeling especially tired and grumpy after a really horrible week at work. When it came time to go to bed, I pulled back our sheets to find a heart-shaped chocolate and two pairs of new socks lying on my pillow—now that's love!

—Matt, married four years to Cyndee

Say How You Feel

Don't assume your partner knows how you feel. Each day, say things like, "I love you, and I'm glad you're mine."

♡

George and I met when we were both widowed with grown children. We thought we had already used up our lives' allotted amount of romance, so when we fell in love, it was like a miracle. It was a second chance at happiness. Even now, we sometimes look at each other across the breakfast table and marvel at our luck. And we say so, all the time, because something so precious should be expressed and not taken for granted.

—Helen, newly married to George

Celebrate!

Make birthdays, anniversaries, and holidays important. Celebrating these special days can be fun and romantic.

We take turns planning something for our anniversary. Last year, I decorated our home after Eric went to bed, and he woke up to find streamers, balloons, and banners everywhere. This year, he planned a surprise day trip. He arranged for a baby sitter, and then took me for a lovely drive to a lake, where we had a picnic and spent the afternoon cloud watching, talking, and dancing to a CD player he brought along. Now I have to think of something to top that wonderful day next year!

—Gail, married five years to Eric

Royalty for a Day

Dedicate one day to pamper your partner like a king or queen. Then have your honey do the same for you.

My family did this as I was growing up, and I brought the tradition to my own family when I got married. We chose half-birthdays as the special days. We scoured a bunch of antique shops to find the perfect dishes, goblet, and silverware for the "royalty" to use. My husband really got into the spirit and found a tiara. Throughout the year, we write down things we might like to do on our days. A few days before my half-birthday, Richard takes my list and plans the day, and vice versa. We've enjoyed breakfast in bed, picnics on the roof, window-shopping for gowns and luxury cars, day trips to nearby towns, and so on. As the kids came along, they got their own prince and princess days, which included visiting the zoo, going on picnics, playing in the sandbox, running under the sprinkler, and so on. The only rule is that we spend the day together, lavishing the royalty with love and affection.

—Donna, married thirty-four years to Richard

Annual Romance

Establish annual romantic traditions that you can look forward to year after year.

We had our first Valentine's Day a few months after we started dating. Jack made me a beautiful card— part drawing, part collage, part poetry. It was the nicest card I had ever received. Since then, every year we've made each other cards instead of giving gifts. We've framed them all. One whole wall in our bedroom is covered with these beautiful symbols of our love.

—Susan, married twenty years to Jack

Daily Romance

Establish daily romantic rituals that bring you together and create stability in your relationship.

♡

In our house, our son instituted "quiet time" on the bed. This means all three of us stop whatever we might be doing and spend up to an hour playing together on the bed. (He doesn't know what quiet *means yet.) Is that romantic? It is for us. If you take three people who love each other, confine them to a small space, and have them tickle and laugh together, you get closeness and enjoyment.*

—Liya, married eight years to Jens

We eat dinner together every night, unless one of us is out of town. Sometimes, though, it's not as simple as it sounds. We both work long and very erratic hours. As a result, we sometimes eat quite late. During one particularly difficult stretch for me at work, Ilya brought in late-night dinners so often that the building's security guard snarled, "You pizza guys have to sign in."

—Stephanie, married six years to Ilya

Modify Traditions

Modify traditions to give them your own personal romantic touch.

ᗰ

Although we both come from families that said grace before every meal, neither of us is particularly religious. Nevertheless, even before our children arrived, we recognized that there was something special about sitting down together for a meal. To commemorate that, we created our own "grace." Before eating, we kissed. That was over thirty years ago, and we still kiss before eating lunch and dinner!

—Barbara and Len, married thirty years

Romantic Meals

Make mealtime a romantic part of your day.

♡

No matter what other craziness is going on in our lives, we always try to make dinnertime special. After spending the day apart, it's therapeutic to do a little manual labor together as we work on a simple meal and then enjoy it face to face. We always listen to the local jazz station at dinnertime; it provides a perfect soundtrack to soothe our work-weary souls and help us focus on each other.

—Christine, married five years to Ron

Hello and Good-bye

Make sure to acknowledge the arrival and departure of the most important person in your life. You don't necessarily have to drop everything and rush to each other's side, but simply show that you notice.

♡

Early in our marriage we began calling out, "Love you!" when one of us came or left home, no matter what arguments we might have had in the meantime. It's wonderful to know that our first or last words to each other will always be loving.

—Anne, married eleven years to Ron

The morning tends to be a little crazy, with my husband going to work and the children heading off to school, but we always kiss and hug before he departs. This simple touch warms my heart, and my day begins with thoughts of welcoming him home.

—Leslie, married sixteen years to Kyle

Couplehood Plus Parenthood

If you have children, try to build your kids into your life; don't build your life around your kids. It's hard to do, but it'll make you happier as a couple and as parents.

We wish someone had given us this advice before our son was born. Our neighbors leave their son with grandparents and baby sitters, and they lead active lifestyles as individuals and as a couple, unencumbered by parenthood. Our friends continue to hike, ski, travel, hunt, and do all their favorite activities with the help of baby carriers. However different their methods, our neighbors and friends enjoy their relationships and share many things of interest other than their offspring. We weren't quite so successful in this regard, so many of our joint hobbies fell by the wayside after the birth of our son, Coby. However, we continued to garden and take walks. It makes us feel like a couple, and Coby's turning out to be quite a gardener and nature lover as well.

—Liya and Jens, married eight years

Translations

Different people say "I love you" in different ways. Learn your partner's language so you can hear "I love you," even when it's not said the way you think it should be said.

ᗡ

I wonder sometimes how I, an extroverted lover of words, ended up with such a stoic. Mark wasn't the husband I dreamed of in my youth—the one who always said the words I needed to hear. In the early years of our marriage, I often felt cheated by Mark's lack of expressiveness. Through the years, I've come to understand that Mark expresses his love for me through acts of service. He helps with the dishes. He takes the kids grocery shopping to give me quiet time. He cooks the bread dumplings my grandfather used to make at family gatherings. Now instead of focusing on his lack of eloquence, I remind myself of his love each time he makes my needs a priority.

—Cory, married seventeen years to Mark

I've learned to look at things from my husband's point of view. Flowers may say "I love you" in my language, but if he washes my car or offers to drive when I'm tired, he says "I love you" in his.

—Sharon, married twenty years to Ken

Love Notes

Leave loving or sexy notes for each other in highly visible places or in unexpected places. Update the messages every week.

I occasionally send my husband love e-mail, but the really special notes are the ones we leave on the refrigerator door. We were married at the Mega Mall (Mall of America), so I address my messages to my "Mega Man" and sign them with "I mega love you."

—Virginia, married six years to Michael

Record the Memories

Keep an album, journal, or scrapbook of your life together to record how your love grows from year to year.

I began a photo journal of the two of us before we got married—photos of our courtship, things we had done, and places we had gone. The album was displayed next to the guest book at our wedding. Ours was a late-in-life marriage, so friends and family enjoyed catching up on our romance through the pictures. I love to page through it now and then, especially when I'm feeling a bit down or upset with my husband. It never fails to make me feel better and put things in perspective.

—Joni, married three years

Love Symbols

Surround yourselves with symbols that bring
back loving, happy memories.

*In our living room, we have a photograph of an
intricate corner of the wooden altar we were married in front of. It looks abstract. Unless we explain
it, no one knows what it is—but we do. We like the
picture, and it's a wonderful reminder of the vows
we took years ago and why we took them.*

—Sara, married eight years

A Picture Says a Thousand Words

Frame your favorite photo of your sweetie. Study it when you need to put your feelings in perspective.

ᗡ

Over the sixteen years of our marriage, we've had some great times as well as some bad times. I was hospitalized for a month before delivering our third child. This long bed rest gave me many hours to think about things. During that time, I often looked at a photo of my husband, Kyle, and reviewed his positive character traits. Kyle is sensitive, smart, strong, and sexy. He's truly my Superman, and reminding myself of this helped me through that long month as well as through other troubles in life.

—Leslie, married sixteen years to Kyle

Real Kisses

When you kiss, do so with your mind and body. Don't think about the dishes or dinner or dusting.

My husband is a really great kisser, and I love the way he'll just grab me and kiss me deeply. We don't care who's around. The kids have grown used to it and pretty much ignore us. Sometimes my mind won't let go of all the things I'm thinking about, but I try to focus on him and the way his kisses make me feel.

—Virginia, married six years to Michael

Skip the Chores

Love and laughter shouldn't fall through the cracks while you do never-ending chores. Every day, put off the lowest-priority chore, and instead use that time to love and laugh together.

We guard our time together ferociously, even when there's a mountain of paperwork to do or dishes to wash or bills to be paid or calls to be answered or social obligations to be met or... well, you get the idea. We know those chores aren't what we want to remember when we celebrate our fiftieth wedding anniversary. We want to look back and think, "What a blast we've had together!" So we carve a little time out of each day and fill it up with "I love you's".

—Christine and Ron, married five years

Laugh It Up

Laughter and loving go hand in hand. Laugh together at every opportunity, and be sure to create plenty of opportunities.

When our son Alexander was born, the first few weeks were overwhelming. Leaky diapers, feedings that lasted one hour out of every three, and the awesome responsibility of caring for this fragile creature left us in a sleep-deprived haze. We kept our sanity (and our unity) by making up increasingly outlandish names for our son: Starvin' Marvin, Filthy Phil, Clean Gene, Gaseous Gus, and our favorite, Goat Boy, after his pitiful bleating. Laughing together took the edge off our irritability, lifted our spirits at a difficult time, and gave us a moment to enjoy each other.

—Stephanie and Ilya, married six years

Spruce Up

Put extra effort into looking nice for each other.

♡

When something was too worn or out-of-date to wear in public, I used to put it aside to wear at home. Then I realized that my husband—the only person whose opinion really counted—saw me pretty much only in my "at-home" clothes. I transferred the at-home pile to the rags pile.

—Pam, married seven years to Stewart

Close the Bathroom Door

Not everything has to be shared. Leave a little mystery in your relationship.

ᗡ

My husband saw me give birth to our two children. We brush and floss our teeth together. We dress and undress in front of each other. But there are some things I want to keep to myself. I feel very strongly that when I go to the bathroom, the door should be firmly closed (although our toddler is usually on my side of the door). When I need to pluck, bleach, shave, and so on, I also close the door or choose a time when my husband isn't home. I want to make sure he can still wonder about the "female" things I do. Preserving a little glamour, a little mystique, takes some effort, but I think it's worth doing.

—Marietta, married eighteen years

Keep Flirting

Flirt, no matter how long you have been
together or how many children you have.

♡

*I flirt with my wife by giving her a glance and
raising one eyebrow as I make sure she sees me
admiring her entire body from head to toe. When
we have guests over or go out with friends, I always
make sure to compliment her publicly. I'll hold her
hand or rest my hand on her leg and look at her in a
way that shows how much I love and desire her.*

—Michael, married six years to Virginia

Better Than Diamonds

Take advantage of the romantic, spectacular shows nature offers you.

Sure, diamonds are terrific, but they're far from being a priority in our household. One of our favorite romantic things to do is look at the stars. We hop in our convertible and drive away from the city and its bright lights that drown out the stars. If it's chilly, we bring a blanket to snuggle under. Then we sit back and watch the skies sparkle.

—Matt and Danielle, married five years

Just a Touch

Touch each other lovingly just to make contact with the one you love.

♡

I learned in the early days of our marriage that Polly has a weakness for attention: She loves it! However, when she feels overwhelmed, she often becomes quiet and withdrawn. I can comfort her and get her to relax just by touching or lightly massaging her hand, shoulders, or back. I don't have ulterior motives (like sex, a return massage, or some complaining of my own), and I know she appreciates that as well.

—Mark, married eighteen years to Polly

Show the World You're in Love

Be affectionate in public. Publicly show how proud and lucky you are to be together.

♡

A couple in our neighborhood still seem to be on their honeymoon, forty years and five children later. I observed them to see what their secret was, and I noticed that they always seem to make eye contact or touch each other—on the hand, arm, shoulder, or back—as they interact. They also genuinely laugh at each other's jokes and do other little things that tell the world they love being together. All these things add up to make a big impression. So, I tried to follow their example. My husband told me he felt more loved when I made those little gestures. They made him feel more confident in himself and our relationship. I thought it was amazing, since my feelings hadn't changed, just how I expressed them. I hope in forty years, other people will study us to figure out what makes our relationship so wonderful.

—Liya, married eight years to Jens

Game Time!

According to the old adage, people who play together stay together. So by all means, be playful.

We love to play games that make us laugh. One of the goofy things we do is have tickling fights, which usually lead to intense, tear-filled laughter. We also love to play Scrabble, attempting to outsmart each other. The challenge is invigorating and fun! At the end, the loser must swallow his or her pride and sing, "You are the champion of Scrabble." It's our quirky addition to the game.

—Chris and Christie, married two years

Go Play Outside

Play outside together to get your blood and adrenaline pumping. A little competition and lots of fun and laughter will energize any relationship.

♡

Too often, as we become adults, we forget that it's okay to have fun. Having a playful, active relationship is one of the true joys of being a couple. In addition to the obvious health benefits, it allows your relationship to grow in a different way. Try as many activities as possible. You'll be amazed at how much you can do together. We enjoy walking, running, in-line skating, water- and snow-skiing, skating, tennis, dancing, golf, playful wrestling, weightlifting, and bike riding, to name a few. Emphasize the fun and laughter, and minimize the competition. This isn't the time to recapture your high-school glory days or exert your dominance. It works best for us to find activities where there's a reasonable degree of parity.

—Brad and Alisa, married two years

Dream a Little Dream

Find time to dream.

♡

For some reason, when the kids are asleep, the music is on, and the fireplace is crackling, we end up kissing and sharing our dreams.

—Matt, married four years to Cyndee

Chapter Four

You're a Team: Share the Good,
the Bad, the Housework,
and the Children

Join in the Fun

Share each other's passions. They'll enrich your life.

D

I've always loved music, but if you'd told me a few years ago that someday I'd be in a band, I'd have said you were nuts. And here I am now, singing in public and playing, of all things, the mandolin! The only reason I am is because seven years ago my husband, Ron, who was "just a friend" at the time, wanted someone to jam with. Pickin' and grinnin' to pass the time in a small town led not only to sharing our music with the public, but also to falling hopelessly in love. Six years later we're still pickin', still grinnin', and more in love than ever.

—"Christine Mae," married five years
to "Ronny Joe"

Gain Strength through Your Struggles

View hardships as opportunities to grow together.

♡

When we were first married, we had no money, a tiny apartment, and no particular prospects. But we had each other, and we had good friends. The laughter and closeness we shared those first years— years in which most people would find little to laugh about—created a foundation for a wonderful life together.

—Carl and Irmgard, married forty years

Compromise Means Respect

There's no relationship without compromise. When two individuals with different personalities, backgrounds, and experiences make a life together, compromise is a great exercise in respect.

♡

My wife and I are stubborn, and for years we'd compromise begrudgingly. Instead of feeling happy that we'd made a decision we both agreed on, we'd feel resentful because we didn't get our respective ways. Then one of our close friends went through a divorce, and she told us to count ourselves lucky. At least we respected each other enough to compromise whenever we didn't see eye to eye. She had spent years with a man who didn't know how to compromise—begrudgingly or otherwise. Seeing her perspective changed ours. We still have times when we feel a compromise means we each "lost" our positions, but we know it's better than losing respect for each other.

—Barry, married twenty-seven years to Carol

They're Not *My* Chores; They're *Ours!*

Don't *help* with the housework and kids; rather, *share* the daily chores. Your home, children, pets, and so on are joint responsibilities.

We're each responsible for certain chores, but as we find ourselves getting busier, sharing responsibilities—such as cooking, cleaning, and yard work—has been both enjoyable and enlightening. It's a way for us to spend time together, and it helps us appreciate the effort it takes to do the chores the other is typically responsible for. When we do a job together, it doesn't feel like such a burden.

—Bill and Vicki, newlyweds

Who Should Do What?

Don't let your preconceived ideas of gender roles determine who does what around the house.

♡

Throughout the first years of our marriage, my husband assumed the household was my responsibility, and I thought so, too. Now on Saturday mornings, we play cards for each chore that needs to be done that week. Everything gets done, no one feels imposed upon, and we became good card players!

—Janet, married twenty-seven years to Michael

Jane and I consider ourselves feminists. However, we don't worry about gender roles in our home life. Instead, we distribute the workload according to preferences and a sense of fairness. Jane cooks, dusts, cleans the bathrooms, and does most of the shopping. I do the dishes, laundry, vacuuming, and most of the outdoor work. We share almost all baby-care duties. We don't worry about which gender does what, as long as the work gets done, the load is shared equally, and no one complains.

—Joe, married five years to Jane

Learning Curve

Ignorance should never be an excuse for avoiding certain household duties. You both should learn how to do nearly every chore.

♡

Since the birth of our third child, my husband has learned to do many new household chores. His help has made a huge difference in our marriage. He still doesn't do laundry, but other than that, there isn't a thing around the house he hasn't learned to do. I've seen a whole new side of him, and it's made me more willing to help him out as well. When we both pitch in, the weekend chores are finished faster, and there's more time for us to spend together as a family.

—Madison, married eight years

Five-Alarm Steak

If you take turns cooking, you're less likely to take the cook and the meal for granted. The same goes for other household chores.

♡

In our first apartment, I set off the smoke alarm every time I broiled steaks. I'd run around, trying to fan the smoke, while the neglected steaks burned under the broiler. Josh, of course, thought my bad luck with steaks was hilarious, and he told everyone we knew about it. I knew he was just teasing, but it still peeved me. Finally, I told him to make the steaks himself to see if he could do any better. He accepted the challenge. Sure enough, beep! beep! beep! *After that, nobody complained about an extra-well-done steak, and Josh started telling everyone that we had a touchy smoke alarm.*

—Angie, married four years to Josh

Loosen Your Grip

Let go of the need to control how a task is completed, and instead acknowledge the effort made to complete it.

When we were both working, we shared the housework. With the birth of our baby, the household became Lara's battleground. Suddenly, putting the dishes in the dishwasher became a task I'd never master to her satisfaction, and using a brush as opposed to a sponge to clean a pan was a point of contention. Finally, we got to the root of the problem: Both of us were adjusting to Lara's new role at home.

—Jacob, married five years to Lara

My sphere of influence shrank significantly when I decided to stay home with our child, and I needed to feel in control of something. Although I wanted Jacob to help with the never-ending housework, he didn't do things the way I'd do them. So I'd redo them irritably and lecture him in the process. Getting our feelings into the open helped me relax my need to control every detail so I could appreciate all that Jacob did around the house.

—Lara

Don't Overconsult

Not all decisions have to be made together. Decide what things require two votes, and leave the other things to executive decision.

Jerry and I each owned a home when we married. We now live together in his house. He has always encouraged my involvement in decorating and upgrading the house. When we purchase major furnishings, we shop together. Although he pays for structural upgrades, such as new fences and landscaping, he always includes me in the planning. But we often purchase accessories, artwork, potted plants, and so on, on our own. At first, we were careful to consult each other, making trips back to stores together when one of us found a treasure that was worth a second look. Then we eventually realized that, since we agreed on most items, it was not worth the second trip for final approval.

—Camille, married seven years to Jerry

Homes Are for Living In

Just as you share a life, you also share a home.
Make your home comfortable for both of you to
live in, not just to look at.

When we moved into our new home, we had a lot of
trouble deciding on furniture. I wanted something
that looked nice, and Chris wanted something
comfortable. We ended up getting an oversize
armchair, which hugged you when you sat down,
and an ottoman. They looked nice and, more impor-
tantly, they were enjoyable to use. Now we can sit
together in our chair-and-a-half, watch movies, and
hold each other for hours.

—Christie, married two years to Chris

Value Means More Than Money

Your value as partners should never be measured in dollars.

♡

When we decided I'd stay home with our first child, I was concerned. It would be the first time in my adult life that I wouldn't earn an income. I knew other women who stayed home and had an allowance for household and personal spending. An allowance! How demeaning. Luckily, we never had any money issues. From the time we began to live together, we pooled our incomes, and the money was always "ours," even though Jens made more than I did. And though I no longer contribute financially, the money is still "ours," not "his." Jens fully realizes that our home depends as much on all I do as on all he earns, and never once has he suggested that I have less of a say because I don't make any money. I think we're very lucky because we value each other and not each other's bank statements.

—Liya, married eight years to Jens

Dream in Tandem

A shared dream, be it a family, a business, or a social cause, will bring you together and give focus to your relationship.

ᗡ

We both agreed early in the marriage that we wanted to provide for our children's education, have a cabin on a lake, and retire as early as possible. We have a very comfortable income, but instead of buying an expensive house and car, as some of our friends have done, we keep focused on our long-term goals. This has made it much easier to prioritize almost everything in our lives.

—Ross and Michelle, married fourteen years

Watch and Learn

Learn from each other. It's flattering for the
teacher and valuable for the student.

ᗡ

*I love to watch my husband interact with people in
his business or in life in general. He talks to people
and makes them feel good about themselves in the
process. He's taught me to be more open with others.
Like him, I now find myself visiting with the
cashier at the grocery store and the retired people at
the park. Because of my husband, a whole new
world is opening up for me.*

—Virginia, married six years to Michael

Chapter Five

Support Each Other: Be Sources of
Strength and Encouragement

Personal Growth

Support each other to achieve personal goals. If you help each other grow as individuals, you'll grow as a couple.

♡

At the beginning of each year, we each write down a personal goal we can achieve with the other's help. Not only does this help us understand each other's desires and goals, but it also helps us depend on and trust in each other to accomplish them.

—Cyndee and Matt, married four years

Taking Turns

Encourage and support each other's goals, even if the process is inconvenient and requires sacrifice.

ᗡ

We had to take turns to achieve a number of personal goals. For instance, when I wanted to take off six months to finish my master's thesis, Sean agreed to support us. When Sean wanted to start his own business, I agreed to take care of everything at home while he moved 150 miles away to set things up. Next, he may move with me so I can work on my doctorate. Even if our goals benefit only one of us directly, our future is stronger if we accomplish them with each other's full support and encouragement.

—Cindy, newly married to Sean

It's Never Too Late

Help each other realize it's never too late to fulfill a dream or goal.

◌

My husband has a graduate degree, but I didn't finish college. So when I decided I wanted to finish twenty years, four kids, and a job later, I was grateful that he found ways to do without my income and to pick up the slack at home while I was at school. My mother waited until she retired at age seventy, and with Dad's wholehearted support, she finished college at age seventy-two and got a master's degree at seventy-four.

—Brenda, married twenty years

The Possibility of a Porsche

If a dream is possible, help make it a reality—even if it's impractical. Impractical doesn't mean unimportant.

ᗡ

I always wanted a classic Porsche for lazy Sunday afternoon drives. This would certainly not be a practical purchase since the car would be old and probably not usable everyday. I talked to Liya about it, and to my surprise, she agreed to open a special savings account for the Porsche. It worked out well, and for quite some time now, we've been enjoying summer Sunday afternoons in our classic car.

—Jens, married eight years to Liya

I can say I initially didn't think buying a Porsche was the best use of our money. However, I could tell how much the car would mean to him, so we decided on a sensible plan to achieve his goal. His pleasure in seeing our Porsche every day, let alone driving it, made the project worthwhile.

—Liya

It's Not a Competition

Celebrate your partner's achievements, big and small. See them as praiseworthy accomplishments, not as reminders of your own shortcomings. Be glad, not jealous or competitive.

I have a high-level job and earn the majority of the income in our family. My husband, Charles, cheers me on to achieve as much as I can at my job. I'm so glad Charles and I see making money as a nice perk, not as something to be jealous or competitive about. Even though this is the twenty-first century, I know several couples whose relationships floundered or failed because the women earned more money than the men and the men couldn't handle it. Charles has always supported me and my career choices, and he's grateful that he can pursue his passion, teaching, without worrying about earning the primary income in our family.

—Rachel, married fifteen years to Charles

Confidence Boost

Be proud of your partner and say so, especially during difficult times and setbacks.

♡

My husband is shy and not as self-confident as he has reason to be. I always told him how proud I was of his accomplishments at work and how I loved that he was so handy around the house—and so handsome. I know he appreciated my comments, even if, unfortunately, he didn't always believe them fully. Later when he was laid off from work, his self-confidence took a heavy blow. The layoff wasn't performance related, but how could anyone not take it personally? I continued to tell my husband how proud I was of all his achievements and how I didn't think less of him in the least. I pointed out that his company's loss would be another's great gain—and it was. We weathered this little storm in our lives, and our relationship became stronger because of the faith and support we showed in and for each other.

—Leah, married nine years

Comfort Zone

Create an oasis of comfort, unconditional love, and encouragement within an unpredictable and frequently disappointing world.

Every morning, my husband makes me a mocha before he goes to work. When I'm sick, he makes me gourmet chicken soup and plain red Jell-O. When I have to teach at night, he'll tape my favorite shows. When I get stuck on a writing project, he'll give me ideas. And when I need a break, he understands— and helps me out. He's a great support, a great father, and a great friend.

—Penny, married thirty years to Tom

Me Time

If your partner has had a bad day or doesn't feel well, offer sympathy, not competition.

I recently went through a period when I was so tired, I was falling asleep at traffic lights. I tried to tell this to my husband, but instead of commiserating and helping me figure out the source of my fatigue, he said, "I haven't been sleeping well either," and went on to talk about himself for ten minutes. I felt misunderstood and trivialized. Finally I asked him for some "me time"—time when I could express my feelings and have him respond without switching the focus to himself. Now he tries hard to support rather an one-up me when I have a problem.

—Darnell, married eleven years to Lee

In Sickness...

Take care of each other when you're sick.

♡

Nancy and I are both really bad at being sick. When I'm sick, for example, she tells me everything I should do, wear, eat, and drink to get healthy. But when she's sick, she does nothing for herself and just walks around feeling miserable. The same is true for me. So we both love knowing that we'll do for each other what we won't do for ourselves. We take turns making gallons of tea, filling hot-water bottles, making each other inhale vile (but very effective) menthol stuff, and so on. I know Nancy will make sure I wear a scarf and jacket, even if I think I can manage without them. And she knows I'll go to the pharmacy in the middle of the night and buy everything that even mildly suggests nighttime relief of her symptoms. Sure, we're both adults, but when I'm sick, I like to know that someone else will take care of me, and I love that she does.

—Aaron, married seventeen years to Nancy

Make Room for Hobbies

Support and encourage your partner's hobbies.

♭

We've always made room in our busy lives for time together as well as time apart to pursue separate avocations (in his case, climbing rocks and frozen waterfalls, and in my case, writing). We're advocates for each other in this regard, providing wholehearted support, even if we don't exactly share each other's adventures. On our convoluted calendar (which includes the demands of two kids and two jobs), we make a point to schedule climbing weekends and an occasional big trip for Bill, and semiweekly writing-group meetings and various conferences for me. We then find time to regroup after our separate trips to share what's happened—at home and "abroad."

—Ann, married fifteen years to Bill

Sing Your Partner's Praises

Give compliments freely for big and little things.

ᗡ

I grew up in a family that was very generous with praise. My husband, on the other hand, didn't. After waiting for him to come around, I decided to take the matter into my own hands. I wrote compliments to myself and left the notes where he was bound to come across them. He would find a note and read out loud, "Jane is a beautiful woman." I'd smile sweetly and say, "Oh, thank you so much!" After a while he got the idea, and now I don't have to leave notes anymore.

—Jane, married fifteen years

Accept the Compliments

Learn how to accept a compliment. Just say, "thank you," and smile.

ᗡ

This has been a tough one for me. From the start, Andre has genuinely complimented me—for the way I look, the things I say, my smile, and so on. But I'd always play down every compliment. I'd tell him he needed glasses, point out that my dress actually made me look fat, or say that my hair was a mess. My reaction frustrated him, and more than once he asked why I couldn't just accept the compliment. He did persevere, and little by little, I began to believe him. Instead of shooting Andre down, I enjoy the fact that he loves me and wants me to know it.

—Sheila, married twelve years to Andre

When Sheila made snide comments about herself when I complimented her, I felt she was saying something bad about the person I loved and about me for loving her. I'm glad I was able to teach her to see herself the way I see her and like herself as I do.

—Andre

Brag a Little

Tell others how wonderful and special your partner is—in your partner's presence. Somehow, words of praise sound different and more flattering when they're said in front of other people.

♡

My wife frequently tells me that she thinks I'm smart, cute, and handy, and I always like it when she does. However, every once in a while, I hear her say something nice about me to a friend, and that feels different—not necessarily better, but somehow stronger, if that makes sense. I mean, it's one thing to comment on something privately, but it's another to remember the thought and voice it a few days later in front of someone else. I always feel great knowing she's so proud of me.

—Jerry, married nineteen years

Mean What You Say

Give only sincere compliments. A compliment from the heart is always appreciated. A hollow compliment is meaningless and simply makes you less trustworthy.

In the first years of our marriage, Frank gave me lots of compliments—for the meals, my hair, the way I looked, the way I kept house, anything. And he meant them. He'd look at me with appreciation when he told me I was beautiful. He'd have a great appetite for the meal he complimented, and then he'd ask for seconds. As the years passed, Frank continued with the compliments out of habit or maybe because he thought I expected them. He'd say I looked nice without even glancing in my direction. He'd comment on the meal while listlessly picking at it with a fork behind the newspaper. They were just words—he didn't mean them, and I no longer believed them. It was almost as if he were lying to me. Instead of giving me pleasure, they just made me feel bad. I should have said something, I guess. But I didn't know what to say.

—Elizabeth, widowed after thirty-seven years

Top-Ten List

Together make a list of the things you're thankful for in your relationship. It'll put your life into perspective and remind you of how much you mean to each other.

♡

After Jane became pregnant with our first child, we established a ritual before bed of making a top-ten list of things we were thankful for. It reminded us how important we were to each other during the challenging transition to parenthood.

—Joe, married five years to Jane

In our busy lives, it's so easy to lose sight of each other and the good things we have and are working toward. Doing this exercise really helps me know how much Joe cares about me and helps us stay connected to the big picture. When we don't do this, too much of our communication ends up being about housework and what needs to get done. I really look forward to making the top-ten list each night. I also learn more about what things I did or said that Joe really appreciated.

—Jane

Thank-You Card

Never miss an opportunity to say how much you appreciate all your partner is and does.

In marriage, sometimes it's easy to forget to say "thank you." My wife is an editor, and she always edited my papers in college, no matter if I finished them at four in the afternoon or four in the morning. At the time, she knew I was appreciative, so perhaps I didn't always say "thank you" out loud. We both knew my thanks was somehow implied. When I graduated, my wife helped me make thank-you cards on our computer to send to family members who attended the ceremony. She didn't realize we printed an extra card. I sent the extra card to her. In it, I made sure to thank her for all of the help she gave me, knowing that there were quite a few times that I had settled for an implied "thank you."

—Josh, married four years to Angie

Chapter Six

Respect Yourself,
Respect Each Other,
Respect Your Relationship

Choose Each Other

Choose each other from the beginning. All conflicts will resolve themselves in the face of your unshakable commitment.

We met on vacation in San Francisco. I was a Jewish-Russian girl from New York. Jens was a German from Germany. We could have chosen to say, "It's been a fun week," and gone to our respective homes to find a nice Jewish boy and a nice German girl. Instead, we decided that little things like history and an ocean should not stand in our way. After we made that decision and managed to get together on one continent, we placed all the other problems that have come up in the course of our marriage in proper perspective.

—Liya, married eight years to Jens

Don't Let Parents Come between You

Respect and honor your parents, but don't let them come between you and your partner. Stick together and stick up for each other.

♡

We met in college and fell in love. Both our families were completely against the marriage; we came from different religions and different economic backgrounds. But we decided being a couple was more important than being a son or a daughter at that stage in our lives. We got married, knowing our families might not speak to us again. Many years and two children later, our families have come around.

—Teresa and Ben, married twenty-five years

Best Friends

Be friends first and foremost. Passion might cool, but friendship will keep you warm forever.

When we first met, I think deep down we both immediately felt a special connection. But (primarily due to an acute case of cold feet suffered by one of us, who shall remain nameless) we took our time getting to know each other over plates of ravioli, on long bike rides, during musical jam sessions, and through a zillion other platonic endeavors. And thanks to all the fun we had before we finally broke down and admitted that we were hopelessly in love with each other, we developed a deep friendship. The mutual respect and playful relationship we've had from the start just grows stronger every day.

—Christine, married five years to Ron

Don't Forget to Be You

Live with, not through or for, your partner. Be an interesting, exciting, independent person in your own right. You'll feel better about yourself, and so will your partner.

When we decided I should stay home after our son Ethan was born, I had less and less to contribute to our conversations. I felt the only thing worth talking about was Matt's job and life. When I joined a moms' organization and began taking classes with Ethan, I was more eager to talk about my day and what I learned.

—Cyndee, married four years to Matt

Staying Healthy

Stay fit together. Not only will you look and feel better, but you'll also have more respect for yourselves and each other.

I think this is one of the most important things a couple can do for each other. I had an uncle who recently died of a heart attack. He weighed around three hundred pounds. His wife was a skinny woman who couldn't deny her husband what he liked so much—eating, and not healthy eating either. He always blamed her for his weight, but he didn't have the willpower or motivation to break the vicious cycle. And so he died, and she was left alone. I wish I could say my wife and I are as serious about exercising as we should be, but with work, four kids, a house... We do, however, encourage each other's exercising efforts, and no matter what, we'll make sure we don't end up like my uncle and his wife.

—Peter, married eight years to Charlotte

Alone Time

Togetherness is wonderful, but not all the time.
Embrace your love, but don't suffocate it.

*When Norris and I moved in together, we saw each
other all the time. It's not that I didn't want to be
with him, it's just that sometimes I needed to be
alone to collect my thoughts, recharge my batteries,
or simply read a book without interruption. At first,
we were afraid to hurt each other's feelings, and we
became a bit smothered by the constant togetherness.
So we talked about it. Now when we need to have
some alone time, we each understand and have our
own activities.*

—Dana, together six years with Norris

Don't Give It Up

Don't give up something you enjoy just because your partner doesn't enjoy it as well.

ᗡ

Although I like some seafood, Liya really loves seafood—not just your middle-of-the-road baked cod, but everything from sushi and caviar to canned oysters. I won't join her when she eats things like oysters, but I'm glad she doesn't give them up on my account. Now that we have a little son who also gobbles up seafood, I've become a minority in our house. Thankfully, nobody has given me a hard time for not joining the other side.

—Jens, married eight years to Liya

No Fennel, Please!

Make a point to know and respect each other's likes and dislikes. Show that you care enough to pay attention to the details.

This advice sums up one of the problems in my first marriage. My ex-wife never really acknowledged my likes and dislikes. For example, I hated fennel (still do), and she loved it. She frequently used it when cooking our meals. When I'd say I didn't like it, she'd simply wave aside my words with, "Don't be silly! How can you not like fennel?" Sure, not liking fennel is a little detail, but it was one of many others she ignored, such as my tastes in wall colors, furnishings, vacations, friends, clothing, and so on. What a difference there is in my second—and last— wife, who actually believes me when I say I don't like something and remembers the things I do like. I love that my needs aren't simply ignored if they're inconvenient.

—John, married three years

Self-Care as Couple Care

Don't neglect your own needs. Sometimes the best way to tend to your relationship is to tend to yourself.

◗

Three years ago, I quit smoking and gained thirty pounds. I always intended to lose weight, but with children, my business, and day-to-day responsibilities, I didn't have time. I let my unhappy and resentful attitude affect everything, including how I treated my husband. Then one day I realized that if I didn't make time for myself, no one else would. I revamped my diet and began to exercise. Now I feel great, I look great, and my attitude toward everything has become wonderfully positive. Once I treated myself right, I could do the same for Jeffrey.

—Genarose, married twelve years to Jeffrey

Lighten Your Load

Don't take on too many personal responsibilities. You won't have time or energy to devote to your relationship.

♡

I'm a stay-at-home mom, and I've always felt the need to justify my role to myself and others. So I took on way too much—volunteer work, favors for friends and family, and a multitude of house-related projects. As a result, I was stressed-out, tired, and irritable to Ross. Somehow in my preoccupation with justifying staying home to take care of my family, I became too busy for my marriage. This year, I decided to cut back drastically on my other responsibilities so my marriage and my kids won't get lost in the shuffle.

—Michelle, married fourteen years to Ross

Your Lips Should Be Sealed

If your partner honors you by sharing a secret, keep it.

ᗝ

Before we married, I shared some of my past experiences with my husband-to-be—private and painful experiences I asked him to keep confidential. About a year into our marriage, my mother-in-law and I were having what I thought was a good discussion about a social issue. At one point, when I thought she was coming around to my way of thinking, she smirked and said, "Of course you think that way. You and your family are nothing but a bunch of losers and drug addicts anyway." She brought this up repeatedly over the next two years to show how she and her family were superior to me and mine. My now-ex-husband never stood up for me or apologized for breaking my confidence.

—Nadine, divorced two years

Say Something Nice

If you need to let off some steam about your partner, turn to a trusted confidant or professional. Speak well of your partner to everyone else.

♡

Do this whenever you talk about your spouse. If there are real negatives in the relationship, then tell your counselor, priest, or other qualified person, not the neighborhood. I can be as sarcastic or cynical as the next person, but when it comes to my spouse, I follow Thumper's advice from Bambi: *"If you can't say something nice, don't say nothing at all."*

—Myra, married two years

There's a woman at my parent-and-child class whose husband I've never met. All I know about him is what she's told me: He's lazy. He's no help around the house. Yet she's been married twelve years to him, and they have three lovely children. I did see him once with his daughter, and he seemed like a nice man who enjoyed being with his child. But I guess she knows better. Or does she? To whom is she doing a disservice by bad-mouthing him—her husband or herself?

—Liya, married eight years to Jens

Maintain Your Standards

Expect the best from each other. High (yet realistic) expectations tend to yield relationships full of respect and love.

When I think about why I love my wife, it isn't simply a matter of who she is with me. I love her because of how she goes about her life at home, at work, everywhere. So if she does something that somehow disappoints me, I'll usually talk to her about it, even if it doesn't affect me directly. For example, she had a tendency to be impatient and sometimes rude to her elderly aunt, who's nice but can talk endlessly about nothing. I pointed this out to my wife. Her initial response was a mix of defensiveness and annoyance, but, ultimately, I think she thought I was right, and she started being nicer to her aunt. I suppose there are people who can love people they don't respect. I don't think I'm one of them.

—Eric, married three years to Rebecca

More Than a Dress Size

Don't ask your partner to change for superficial reasons.

ᗞ

Before I got married, I was always on a diet, trying to be as skinny as my boyfriends wanted me to be. I didn't marry any of them, though. Instead, I married the man who loved me for me, and not for my dress size.

—Grace, married two years

Don't Take Advantage

Don't take advantage of each other. The short-term advantage will never outweigh the long-term damage to trust, respect, and self-esteem.

During the first year of our marriage, my husband's vacation was scheduled when I was seven months pregnant. I didn't feel up to going, but I insisted that he go alone. (I knew he worked hard and needed this vacation.) He had a great time and decided he would vacation on his own every year. Deep down, I didn't support his decision, but I didn't have the confidence to contradict it. He took advantage of my inability to stand up for myself. So he vacationed alone, and I had to vacation with first one, then two children. Once the pattern was set, he didn't want to change it, and I didn't know enough to try.

—Paula, divorced after thirteen years

Old Flames

Discussing or asking about past relationships will likely be uncomfortable. Leave past relationships where they belong: in the past.

My wife and I are from different countries and religious backgrounds. Her former boyfriends are from her background, which always makes me feel a little inadequate. Naturally, she married the best of the bunch (me), but I still don't appreciate hearing stories about them, even something as innocent as her mother meeting one of them at the market. Liya knows how I feel, and when the former boyfriends are mentioned, we have an unspoken agreement that I can make fun of them and point to her good judgment in choosing me as her husband. This kind of discussion usually closes the subject quickly while leaving us both in a good mood.

—Jens, married eight years to Liya

Unique Retreats

It's comforting to have a place to call your own.
Respect each other's personal spaces and retreats.

♡

*Colin and I decorated our house together. Fortunately,
we have similar tastes, so we didn't have too much
trouble with our shared living spaces. However,
each of us got a special room, which we could do
with as we pleased. My small den is very feminine
and filled with all the things I love. (Colin would
say it's cluttered—if he had a say.) Colin's space has
wall-to-wall cars and trucks and a large-screen
television. (I'd say it's decorated by a fifty-something
boy who refuses to grow up—if I had a say.) I love
my personal space, especially because it's so completely and uniquely mine, and Colin feels the same
about his room. We're each welcome to visit the
other's retreat, as long we keep our opinions to
ourselves.*

—Evaline, married twenty-one years to Colin

Thoughtful Gifts

You might not pick a winner every time, but try to buy thoughtful gifts for your partner. No one likes to receive presents that miss the mark.

For my thirty-fifth birthday, my husband decided to give me a special gift. He presented me with a gold chain and matching bracelet, valued well over a thousand dollars. I appreciated that he wanted to give me something nice, but I don't buy or wear jewelry, so the price was a lot higher than the value to me. I could think of plenty of other ways to spend that money. We ended up returning the jewelry. Instead, he gave me a thirty-dollar oscillating fan for my gym, which I love.

—Anne, married twelve years to Ron

Work Is Important

Value each other's work. It's a big part of your identity and takes up huge portions of your life.

ᗯ

From the very beginning, my husband let me know that his work was more interesting, important, and difficult than mine. He frequently commented that my job wasn't important and that anyone could do it. First I got angry. When that changed nothing, I became very disappointed in him and in our relationship. I stopped telling him anything about my work, and then anything at all.

—Sabine, separated after five years

Joy of Giving

Give more than you take.

♡

My boyfriend, Jay, is a very generous, selfless person, while I'm self-centered. Jay is patient when I make a mistake or get moody. I, on the other hand, am quick to criticize. Jay offers support or a helping hand without me having to ask for it. I, on the other hand, usually need to be asked two or three times before I help—even then, I help with a great deal of complaining. It's not that I don't respect or love him. I'm just afraid that if I don't look after my best interests, no one will. Of course, that's a ridiculous thought. Jay will always look after my best interests, and I should do the same for him. That's what it means to be in a relationship. Giving comes naturally to Jay, and I admire him for that. The longer I'm with him, the more I'll learn to set my self-centeredness aside so I can give him as much as—if not more than—he gives me.

—Tamika, together with Jay five years

The Importance of Trust

Trust and be trustworthy. Keep your promises.

ꕤ

I grew up in a family with two shining examples of exactly how not to be trustworthy. My father and my brother both thought nothing of promising what would make you happy in the short term or would simply get you off their backs: "Sure I'll come home in time for dinner." "Absolutely, I'll take you to the airport." "Of course I'll call while I'm out of town so you don't worry." Those and hundreds of other promises were never kept over the years. Nobody in the family trusted or counted on them. We all knew their words were just air. That knowledge was painful and disappointing. As a result, I've never made a promise I knew I couldn't keep—not even a little white lie that probably wouldn't have mattered to anyone. I know my husband and family can count on me, and I carry the weight of that responsibility with pride.

—Linda, married twenty-two years

Share the Spotlight

When faced with a choice between making your-self or your partner look good, don't choose your-self. Kindness is always better than selfishness.

When my husband and I went out with friends during the first years of our marriage, I'd work hard to show him and everyone else how fun and clever I was. What I didn't stop to notice was that my husband felt left out and overshadowed. To retaliate or simply to get some attention for himself, he began to flirt with other women. If I'd drawn him into the group rather than made myself look good, we'd have both won. Instead, we entered a destructive cycle that didn't end well for either of us.

—Paula, divorced after thirteen years

Let Your Partner Shine

Don't rain on your sweetie's parade.

♡

I have a friend who consistently rains on his wife's parade. If she begins a joke, he interrupts to say he's heard it already. If something good happens to her, he finds at least one reason why it shouldn't have happened or how it's actually a bad thing for someone else. I've asked him why he does this, but he either laughs it off as my imagination or assures me that he's just "helping her get the facts straight." In the meantime, my wife and I both observed that his wife speaks less and less in his presence and is a lot less lively than she was just a year ago. I'm not a betting man, but if I were, I wouldn't put anything on this couple's longevity.

—Someone who wishes he could do more

Be Faithful

If you think you might ever be tempted by someone other than your spouse, have a sure-fire method to keep yourself from straying.

ᗡ

Before we got married, my wife told me our relationship would end if I cheated on her. (Actually, she said she would make very sure I wouldn't ever cheat again—and I'll skip the gory details.) That was the last time she said anything on the subject. I don't know if she remembers saying that, but I never forgot it. In the years since then, I have jokingly related her threat to women who seemed interested in more than friendship. It has worked wonderfully to remind me of my priorities and to get me out of potentially uncomfortable situations.

—Shelley, married thirty years

Kill the Green-Eyed Monster

Trust and jealousy are mutually exclusive.
Choose trust.

ᗠ

*I'm a very social and affectionate person. My wife
knew that before we got married. One of the things
I love best about our marriage is that she has never
nagged, questioned, or in any way behaved jealously
over the years. She trusted me to know where my
priorities lay. Even if I joked or flirted with other
women, I always knew where home was, and that
was with my wife. I could always come home safely,
without repercussions. I'm not saying I was right in
my behavior, but I love my wife for hers.*

—Boris, married thirty years

The Greatest Sacrifice

Share the little things you'd ordinarily want for yourself, even if your partner doesn't know about your sacrifice.

♡

Jens and I both like the end pieces on a loaf of bread best. Whoever makes the sandwiches gives the end pieces to the other, and we always notice and appreciate the gesture. We also both love chocolate. When I scoop ice cream into bowls and get a big batch of chocolate chips in one scoop, I always (okay, almost always) put that scoop into Jens's bowl. He doesn't always know it, but I do. Sure, it's a little thing, but as I sacrifice that chocolate-laden scoop, I know I'd only do that out of love—strong love. That reinforces in a small but concrete way my feelings for my husband.

—Liya, married eight years to Jens

Chapter Seven

Know and Accept Yourself
and Each Other for Better
and for Worse

Take the Whole Pie

Accept the entire package that is your partner.

♡

Whenever I want my husband to change, I remind myself that if I cut a slice out of a pie, the pie isn't whole anymore. For instance, his inflexibility sometimes drives me crazy, but I love his stability. They're related. I have to put up with one if I want the other.

—Sharon, married twenty years to Ken

Complementary Personalities

Enjoy your differences. Would you really like your partner to be just like you, with all your positive and negative qualities?

♡

We've noticed a classic difference between us: I like to live in the present, whereas Pete tends to dream about and plan for the future. Sometimes this can cause friction when I feel cleaning the house is more important than revising the latest house plans.

—Teri, married six years to Pete

However, realizing this, we make a great team. Without me our future would be happenstance, and without Teri our present would be chaos. Teri keeps me more grounded in the present, and I help her look to the future.

—Pete

Whom Did You Marry?

Love your partner, not your partner's potential.

ᗪ

When we said "I do," I knew whom I married. In hindsight, however, I'm not sure whom my wife-to-be promised to honor and cherish. In the years that followed, it became clear it wasn't me. She decided I was a diamond in the rough she would polish. The problem was that I didn't want to be nudged or pushed according to her design. I was doing what I was doing because I liked it, not because I needed her help to "improve" myself.

—Brandon, divorced after seven years

When I fell in love with Michael, he was a smoker. I thought Michael would stop smoking after we were married. I soon realized that the more I nagged, the more he smoked. Instead of sounding like his lover, I sounded like his mother. That thought stopped me cold. I accepted his habit, and we went about our life. A couple of months later, Michael came home and announced he was going to stop smoking. True to his word, he's now a nonsmoker.

—Virginia, married six years to Michael

Reality Check

Your relationship isn't a romance novel. Adjust your expectations accordingly, and learn to appreciate reality.

In high school, I read hundreds of Harlequin novels, and I knew my perfect mate would be tall, dark, and handsome. His wavy hair would tumble above a Greek profile. He'd anticipate my every wish and give me foot rubs every night. The man I married turned out to be medium height, redheaded, and cute. Jens's coppery hair doesn't tumble but instead recedes above his freckled profile. He doesn't anticipate my every wish, but he's happy to fulfill my wishes when I tell him what they are. He gives decent foot rubs, but more importantly, he makes me laugh when I need it most, supports anything I wish to accomplish, and is the best possible father to our children. Each year, my husband grows more handsome, and I couldn't have imagined his equal, no matter how many romance novels I might have read.

—Liya, married eight years to Jens

It Could Be Worse

Not everything will please you. Concentrate on the things that do please you, and learn to let go of those that don't.

♡

Some of my married friends complain that their husbands don't help with chores enough or that they watch too much television. Sure, those things can be annoying, but I say we should put them in perspective. One of my ex-husbands was an alcoholic. I know what a bad situation looks like. Now I have a husband who's a keeper, and we love and respect each other. And if he forgets to take out the garbage or spends Sunday glued to the TV, so what?

—Margaret, married ten years to Gary

Little Quirks

Notice the little things that make your honey unique.

♡

Jürgen refuses to go to the barber. He insists on cutting his hair himself. He knows how to work a computer, but he's totally helpless reading the instructions for his cell phone. He won't leave the house without an undershirt, but he won't wear his pajama bottoms at night. He may not be perfect, but he's mine.

—Martina, together nine years with Jürgen

Matt has a unique talent for losing his glasses. I, on the other hand, have a unique talent for finding them.

—Cyndee, married four years to Matt

Look on the Bright Side

You'll usually see what you expect or want to see. Practice looking for the positive.

♡

When my husband and I were having problems with our teenage son, it became very difficult for me to see anything but our problems. I'd wake up in a bad mood, expecting problems and always finding some. After going on a crying jag, I decided enough was enough. One negative thing, however big, shouldn't spoil everything else, including my marriage. I needed to spend more time appreciating the good things in my life and less time concentrating on the bad. To change, I started each day by thinking of five positive things I was grateful for. This allowed me to put things in perspective and start to feel better about myself and my life. After talking about it, my husband and I came up with a list of things we could learn from our ordeal. I might sound like Pollyanna, but it helped us make it through a difficult time.

—Anya, married thirteen years

Strengths and Weaknesses

Know your strengths and your weaknesses, and be sure to recognize which are which.

ᗡ

I guess I'm a neat freak. I was always proud to be so organized and clean, until I moved in with my boyfriend. Then it became a problem. It's not that Gerry was a lazy slob—he just wasn't as anal about everything as I was. That's something I can say now with hindsight. At the time, it drove me crazy and nearly broke us up. When I was seriously considering moving out, Gerry sat me down and asked what would happen if we washed the floor only once a week instead of every day, or if we put away the newspaper at the end of the day instead of the second I closed the last page, or if we washed the dishes after eating instead of while cooking. I realized nothing would come crashing down around my head. So we made some ground rules we were both comfortable with. And I didn't leave. I married him instead.

—Alison, married fifteen years to Gerry

Know When to Hold 'Em

A hug can fix many things, so know when to give one.

♡

Josh and I dated in high school, and only a few months into our relationship, my family's dog died. I called Josh, in tears, to tell him the news. A few minutes later, Josh appeared with two cartons of chocolate milk and a bag of Oreos. We sat on my front steps and ate a few cookies, then Josh hugged me while I cried. "Milk and cookies always make things better," he later explained. True, the cookies did help, but the hug made the real difference. That hug said Josh cared enough to comfort me and share my pain.

—Angie, married four years to Josh

Know When to Leave 'Em Alone

Notice if certain situations trigger your honey's bad moods. Giving him or her a little space during these times will improve everyone's mood.

I'm not a morning person, to put it mildly. My husband learned the hard way that expecting me to be at all lively before I've taken my shower isn't in anybody's best interest. So now he wisely leaves me to my morning routine and waits until I signal with a good-morning kiss that I'm ready for the day. Our mornings have become significantly more peaceful and pleasant, which tends to spill over into the rest of the day.

—Liya, married eight years to Jens

Know Your Limits

If you can't do it, hire someone who can.

♡

Rich thinks if he's capable of fixing something, there's no reason to pay someone else to do it. The problem is that sometimes he can't fix everything or he's too busy to do the job in one chunk of time. So we wind up with half-wallpapered rooms or disassembled objects lying around for weeks or even months, which is frustrating. After a number of years, I decided that when we have a job Rich thinks he can do himself, he has a week to do it. After that, I hire a professional.

—Madeline, married fifteen years to Rich

I was raised to value hard-earned money and to spend it judiciously. If I know I can do something myself, I hate paying someone else to do it. But I'm also busy. Madeline's solution actually gave me a graceful out. Yes, I still believe in not wasting money. But I also believe that maybe I should value time more than money—especially time spent enjoying my wife and kids instead of worrying and arguing about unfinished projects.

—Rich

Can't Buy Me Love

Money won't make your partner sexier, smarter, wittier, or more understanding, and it won't make you happier.

♡

An unlimited supply of money can help a lot of things, but true love and affection can't be bought. Some people earn a lot of money and then use it to lavishly decorate their partners with diamonds, expensive watches, and so on. They serve each other's egos and exhibit their wealth. Those are certainly the wrong values to prioritize in a relationship. True love isn't based on wealth but on accelerated heartbeats when you see your partner—and those come free of charge.

—Jürgen, together nine years with Martina

Embrace Change

Every relationship constantly evolves as the people in it mature, learn, and change. Fighting to keep things the same is a losing battle. Accept and embrace the evolution.

We married and started a family when we were still teens. Since then, we've each earned degrees, built careers, raised and educated five children, and cared for and buried our parents. We're now adjusting to retirement together. It's not easy. But even if we bicker and complain sometimes, we recognize this new phase in our lives as an opportunity for growth...again.

—Tom and Ruth, married forty-two years

We lived in New York, where I had been my whole life. We both had jobs and friends, and the kids had day care they liked. Then Jim was offered a too-good-to-pass-up job in North Carolina. We decided to try it for two years. I was never so scared in my life, but am I ever glad we made that decision. Our home may not be in a metropolis, but we've discovered sides of ourselves we didn't know existed—good sides. Ten years have passed, and nobody is talking about going back to the Big Apple.

—Eleanor, married sixteen years to Jim

The Grass Is Never Really Greener

Nobody has a perfect relationship. Every couple has something they would change if they could. So don't waste your time envying others' relationships. Instead, work hard on your own.

My husband has some habits that drive me up the wall. When I was up that wall, I used to think about couples who seemed to have perfect relationships— they went out, had fun, went on trips together, Rollerbladed, and laughed a lot. And then one of the couples got a divorce because they had incompatible life goals. Then I found out that another couple has been trying to have a baby for the last five years, and that they would gladly trade their free-and-easy lives for my two o'clock feedings and diaper duty. And yet another friend confided that she wished her husband could be half as helpful around the house and as patient with the kids as mine is. So I climbed off my wall, hugged my husband, and told him how lucky I was to have him. And on that wall I hung a picture of our family.

—Lauren, married eighteen years

Also from Meadowbrook Press

✦ *52 Romantic Evenings*
Unlike other romance books that provide only brief outlines of ideas, this book provides everything a couple needs to know to create romantic evenings that will make their relationship come alive. It details complete plans for a year's worth of romance-filled dates, including where to go, what to wear, what to eat, what to drink, what music to play, and more.

✦ *Create a Date*
Here are 52 ideas for fun, relaxing, romantic, and sexy dates guaranteed to add life to your relationship, emphasizing activities couples can do together, rather than for one another. *Create a Date: Book Two* features 52 more exciting and relationship-enhancing activities, specially designed to bring partners closer.

✦ *Reflections for Newlyweds*
The daily reflections in this book illuminate every turn in the newlyweds' journey together and nurtures them through the ups, downs, and in-betweens of their new love.

We offer many more titles written to delight, inform, and entertain. To order books with a credit card or browse our full selection of titles, visit our web site at:

www.meadowbrookpress.com

or call toll-free to place an order, request a free catalog, or ask a question:

1-800-338-2232

Meadowbrook Press • 5451 Smetana Drive • Minnetonka, MN • 55343